Let the Fun Begin!

This booklet is a treasure chest of ideas, ranging from cool costumes to tips on face painting and fashioning accessories. The patterns included make the easy-to-finish projects come together even faster. Even if you've never made a costume for your child before, the photos and easy-to-follow step-by-step instructions will teach you what you can create with a piece of wire and a twist of the wrist.

You'll soon learn the types of material available in most fabric stores (or even at the back of your closet) are enough to spark your imagination for countless costume creations. Work from scratch or in layers, adding on to existing foundation clothes, and then choose accessories to add that all-important touch of magic or ghoulish detail. In no time, you'll be a master of Halloween dress and theatre wardrobes!

Radiatex, a polyester padding with a metallic-colored finish, is a sturdy and easy-to-cut covering for aspiring robots. Flashy fringe, spiralled two-tone cord, and a rainbow of ribbons and feathers make your Halloween palette unlimited.

Flexible, colorful, and strong, pipe cleaners support as well as decorate.

Nothing puts the flash in a cape or regal robe like red satin. This 100% acetate lining does the trick economically.

Plush, printed fabrics with feline stripes and spots are just the thing for the wild at heart.

From the extra large to the delicate and petite, buttons, beads, and decorative tunic hooks 'do up' costumes for princes and clowns.

Sheer, light-weight, and easy to shape, tulle is the ideal material for anything from a crinoline underdress to a ballerina's tutu.

The sturdy thickness of felt permits irregularly-cut shapes—a good choice for tunics, collars, and hats.

Frightfully real, plastic and rubber creepy crawlers make that costume come alive!

Dandy Disguises

This section showcases an array of imaginative costumes, some made in minutes with cast-off garments, and others that involve fabric, scissors, and a glue gun. Plunder closets and local thrift shops for special touches: a weathered fedora for a private eye, an eye patch and bandana for a pirate, and jazzy jewelry for a roaring twenties beauty.

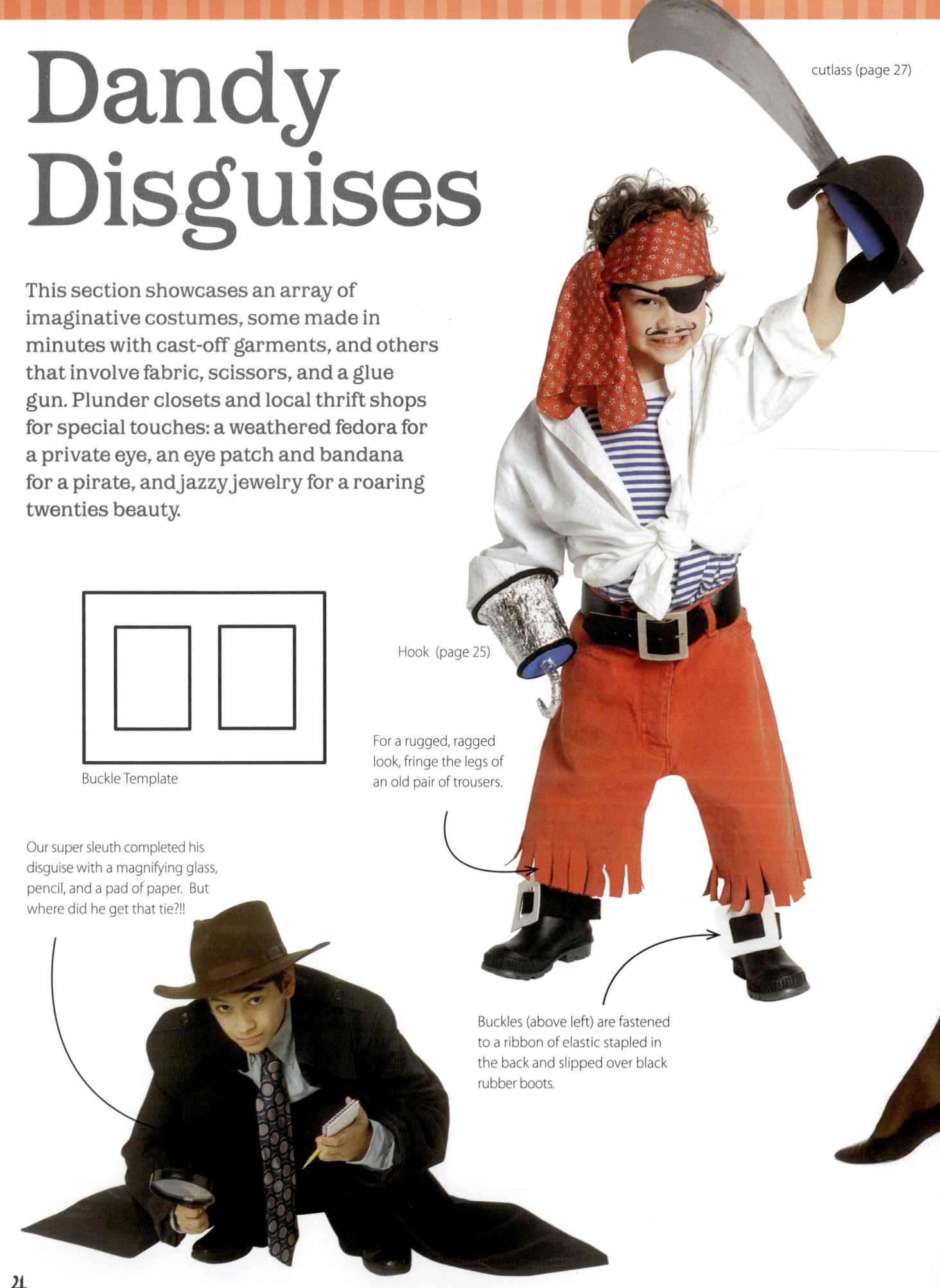

cutlass (page 27)

Buckle Template

Hook (page 25)

For a rugged, ragged look, fringe the legs of an old pair of trousers.

Our super sleuth completed his disguise with a magnifying glass, pencil, and a pad of paper. But where did he get that tie?!!

Buckles (above left) are fastened to a ribbon of elastic stapled in the back and slipped over black rubber boots.

A spooky face painted on a sheet enhances this ghost's disguise. The bandana around her neck holds the eye and mouth holes in place so she can always breathe comfortably and see clearly.

Beads, a bandana, a paisley shirt, and—above all—a laid-back attitude are all this flower child needs to show she's hip. For tips on face painting see page 16.

This fabulous flapper has dressed to please herself. The dress was a lucky find, but any long-waisted dress will do, especially when set off by a feather boa and long beads. Her headband—a signature fillip for 1920 party girls—is decorated with a gaudy brooch and a matching feather.

Don't forget to...

- Check with the grown-ups before raiding their closets; sometimes it's difficult to distinguish between a cast-off and a rarely used, but treasured, item.
- Make sure you can see clearly and breathe comfortably—whatever the disguise.
- Keep small objects, like beads, balloons, and hard candy, from younger friends who might choke on them.
- Take care using long scarves, necklaces, and anything else that you wear around your neck.
- Adjust long dresses, oversized pants, and adult shoes so that you don't trip and hurt yourself.

Capes & Cloaks

YOU'LL NEED:

Materials for cape/cloak:
- Fabric
- Ribbon

Tools:
- Scissors
- Glue gun

Superheroes, vampires, royalty, and magicians are just a few of the fabulous characters who depend on a cape or a cloak for authenticity. Fortunately they're easy to make; just cut and glue as we've shown here. Shop for remnants or use scraps of old fabric, choosing a material that hangs in soft folds.

Face paint (page 16) instead of a mask was used here to make it easier to see when trick or treating.

This tunic, like Robin Hood's (page 9), is made of felt. The side seams are glued together. The emblem "S," also felt, was glued to poster board before being attached to the front.

The belt is a piece of fabric folded lengthwise, threaded through a felt buckle (pattern, page 4), and secured in the back with a safety pin.

1 Fold a large rectangular piece of fabric in half. We used a 28"x 56" (711 x 1422mm) piece of red jersey for this superhero's cape.) For the neck, cut a quarter circle from one folded corner. Then cut a long connecting curve between the two opposite corners, as shown.

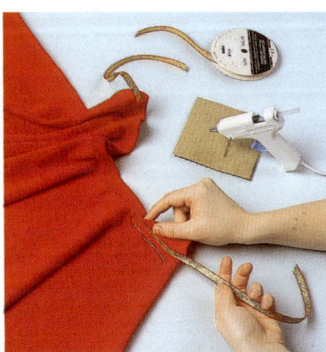

2 Cut a piece of ribbon about a yard (meter) in length and lay it along the collar. Fold a hem over the ribbon (make sure that the hem is wider than the width of the ribbon) and glue the edge down.

Count Dracula's face and hair (page 17) took less than a half hour to create.

The count's cloak is made in the same way as the superhero's (facing page)—but it is longer and has a stand-up collar.

YOU'LL NEED:

Material for stand-up collar:
- Fabric (red and black)
- Wire hanger
- Electric tape

Tools:
- Pliers
- Scissors
- Glue gun

Tip:
Curving the count's collar around the back of the head will help keep it standing.

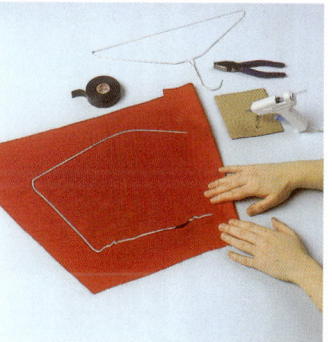

1 For the count's collar, bend wire from a clothes hanger into the shape of a pentagon. Tape the wire ends together with electric tape. Wrap one side of the wire in red fabric and glue down the edges.

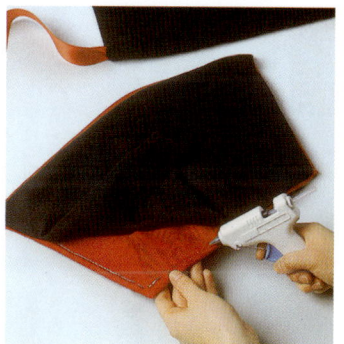

2 Cover the other side of the coat hanger in black fabric, leaving a couple of inches to overhang along the bottom. Bend the red side inward. Glue the overhang to the neck of the cloak, so that the black side faces out.

Terrific Tunics

Gallant knights, medieval princes, archers, Native American princesses, and a slew of superheros don tunics when they dress for Halloween. Our knight is sporting a tunic made from a pillow case. Robin Hood, on the other hand, is wearing one cut from felt. Choose colors in keeping with the role—for example, bright colors for superheros, more somber ones for knights—and don't forget the hat (pages 12–13) and other accessories (pages 24–25).

Make the helmet as shown on pages 12–13. Wrap it in aluminum foil and glue a piece of rubber drawer liner around the rim for mail. The rest is up to you.

Sword (page 24)

This knight's chain mail is made of rubber drawer liner. Tie the liner to the forearms and shins with string threaded through the mesh.

Shield (page 25)

1 To make a tunic from a pillowcase, mark the openings for the arms and head with tape. Cut along the tape.

2 Every knight should bear an escutcheon or coat of arms on his tunic. We cut ours out of a royal blue pot scrubber in the shape of a shield, decorated it with gold and blue ribbons, and trimmed it with gold rope ribbon and black pipe cleaners.

YOU'LL NEED:
Materials for knight's tunic:
- Large pillowcase
- Masking tape
- For the escutcheon; pot scrubber, ribbon, rope ribbon
- For the chain mail; rubber drawer liner
- String

Tools:
- Glue gun
- Scissors

Tip:
Robin Hood's arrows are glued into the quiver to keep them from falling out.

Cap (page 13)

Quiver, bow, and arrows (page 24).

A Tunic for Robin Hood

You'll need: green felt, suede ribbon, scissors, and a glue gun.

1. Cut a piece of forest green felt that is the width of Robin Hood's shoulders and twice the length between shoulders and knees.
2. Fold the fabric in half lengthwise and cut a hole in the middle of the fold for the head.
3. Cut a fringe at the shoulders and knees.
4. Make a fancy collar with triangles of light and dark green felt and suede ribbon—the same ribbon can be used as a belt.

9

Boxes & Boards

Sandwich boards and boxes form the basis of many fanciful costumes from Jack-in-the-box to the Queen of Hearts, from robots to dice. It all depends on your cunning choice of decorations. Our Pizza Girl comes dressed with a yummy variety of tasty tidbits made from felt, rubber, and paper cut in the shapes of mushrooms, pepperoni, green peppers, olives, and cheese.

Make the chef's hat with scored white poster board rolled into a cylinder and secured with glue. Use white cotton stuffed with craft fill for the crown.

YOU'LL NEED:
Materials for Pizza Girl Costume:

- Red foamcore
- Unbleached cotton
- Craft fill
- For pizza dressing, use scraps of fabric, bits of rubber, whatever strikes your fancy.

Tools:

- Craft knife
- Brown marker
- Glue gun

Tips:

- Only use a craft knife under adult supervision.
- Only use a hot glue gun under adult supervision.

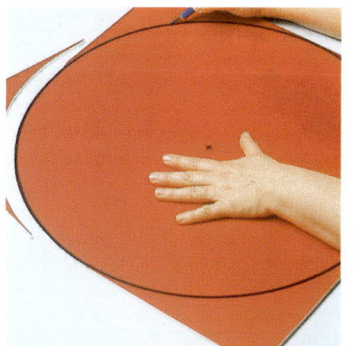
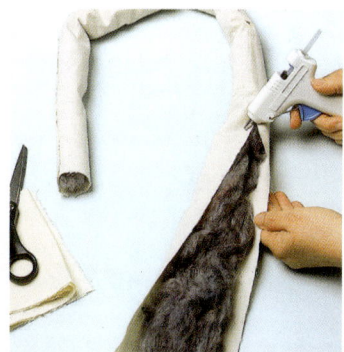
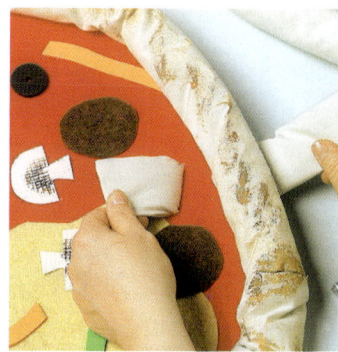

1 Outline the pizza shape on two pieces of foamcore. We used 20" x 20" (508 x 508mm) pieces of red foamcore. Cut them out with a craft knife.

2 Wrap and glue long pieces of unbleached cotton around craft fill to make the crust. Glue the fabric rolls around the edge of the foamcore pieces and touch them up with brown marker or paint.

3 Now cut out shapes of your favorite toppings and glue them on. Make two more rolls of craft fill wrapped in cotton for the shoulder straps. Slip the ends through slits in the foamcore and glue the ends to the surface.

A Box for a Robot

You'll need: A large box for the body shell, dryer tubing, electric wiring, rubber bath mat, choice of decorations, and metallic silver spray paint.

Face Painting (Page 16)

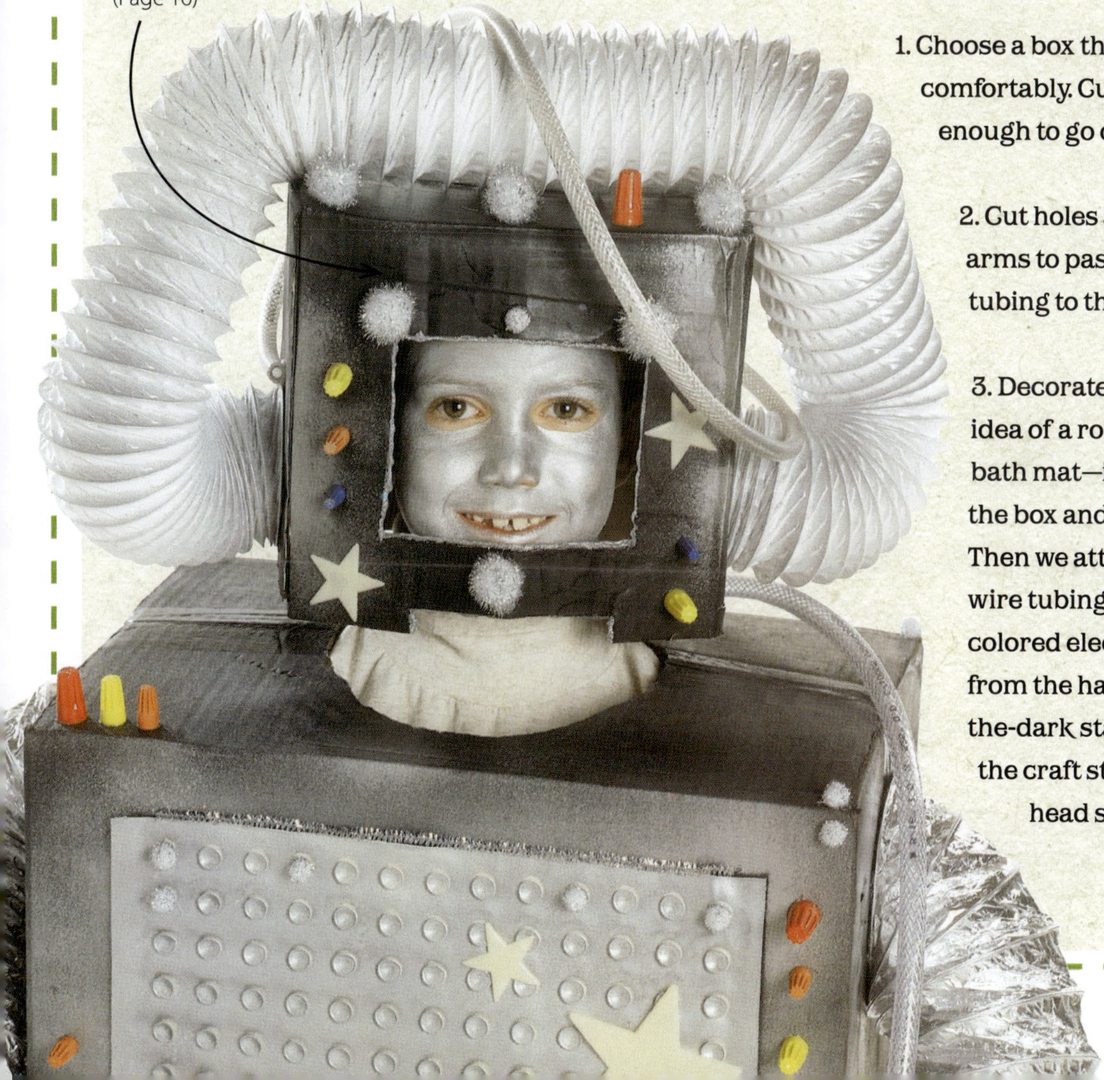

1. Choose a box that is large enough to wear comfortably. Cut out an opening big enough to go over the head easily.

2. Cut holes at the right height for the arms to pass through. Glue dryer tubing to the arm holes.

3. Decorate the box to resemble your idea of a robot. We glued the rubber bath mat—inside out—to the front of the box and then spray painted it silver. Then we attached pieces of plastic wire tubing here and there and added colored electrical wire connectors from the hardware store. The glow-in-the-dark stars and balls came from the craft store. For tips on making the head shell, see page 13.

Hatter's Heaven

The hat lies at the heart of most great disguises. Magicians and matadors sport cylindrical hats. Witches and damsels—in distress and otherwise—are known for their cone-shaped hats. As for robots, the hat of choice is a box, cut and decorated with flair.

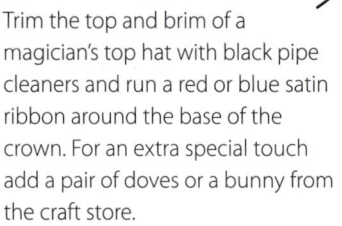

Trim the top and brim of a magician's top hat with black pipe cleaners and run a red or blue satin ribbon around the base of the crown. For an extra special touch add a pair of doves or a bunny from the craft store.

Create a festive witch's hat with orange rice paper and golden stars.

YOU'LL NEED:

Materials for Witch's Hat:
- Black poster board
- Orange rice paper
- Gold stars

Materials for Magician's Top Hat:
- Black poster board
- Ribbon
- Pipe cleaners
- Pair of doves

Tools:
- Pencil
- String
- Scissors/craft knife
- Tape
- Glue gun

Witch's Hat

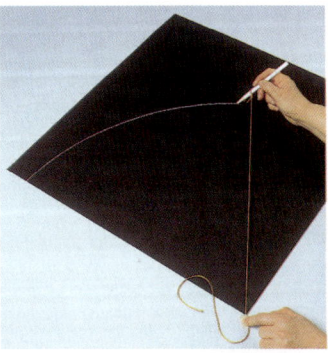

1 To make a cone hat, outline a quarter circle on poster board with string. For a witch's hat use a 21" (533mm)-long string. Cut along the line. Roll into a cone and lightly tape the sides together. Adjust the hat to fit before securely gluing or taping the sides together.

2 Stand the cone on another piece of board and trace around the cone. Draw a second circle 3" (76mm) outside the first. Cut along this line. Draw a third circle 1" (25mm) inside the first circle and cut along the line. Then cut slits to the first line to make a 1" (25mm) fringe, as shown above.

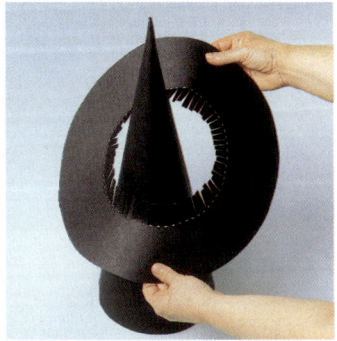

3 Slide the brim over the cone. Glue the fringe to the outside of the cone. Decorate it as you wish. Adding a band of wide ribbon will hide the glued fringe seam.

Magician's Top Hat

1 Make a medium-sized cylinder hat by rolling a rectangular piece of poster board about 9" x 24" (229 x 610mm) into a cylinder and gluing or taping the sides together. Roll it tighter if it is too big. Make a brim as described on facing page (step 2).

2 Cut a circle in poster board that has a diameter 2" (51mm) longer than the diameter of the cylinder. Cut a 1" (25mm) fringe around the circle and insert it into the top of the cylinder as shown. Glue the fringe to the inside of the cylinder.

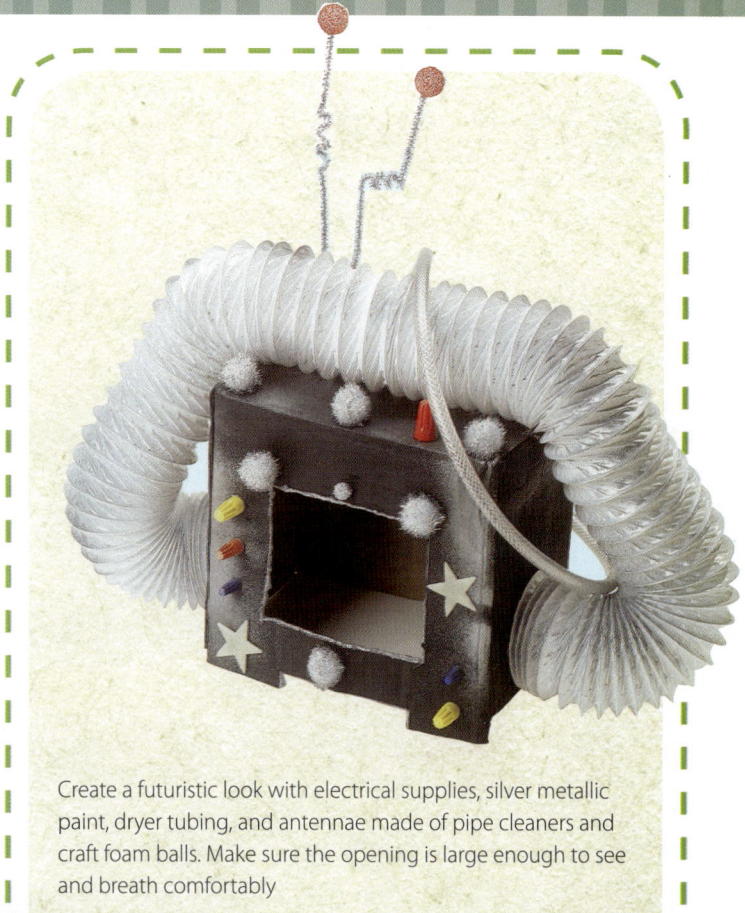

Create a futuristic look with electrical supplies, silver metallic paint, dryer tubing, and antennae made of pipe cleaners and craft foam balls. Make sure the opening is large enough to see and breath comfortably

Consult patterns and instructions on page 28 for making Robin Hood's cap. Decorate it with suede ribbon and a feather.

To make the knight's helmet, follow the instructions on facing page (step 1) but use a 10" (254mm)-long string instead.

13

Mask Parade

Wear a flashy mask to your next ghoulish gathering or turn mask-decorating into a party activity for your guests. Patterns for the masks shown here are at the back of the booklet. Cut them out and go to town decorating them with items found in a well-stocked craft box—paint, sequins, sparkles, pipe cleaners, felt, feathers, yarn, and craft foam balls.

1 Trace the mask (pattern, page 30) on a sheet of poster board. Cut it out, using a craft knife to cut the openings for the eyes.

2 Paint the mask to your liking. Let each color dry thoroughly before applying the next one. You may want to experiment on a sample before beginning to work on the real mask.

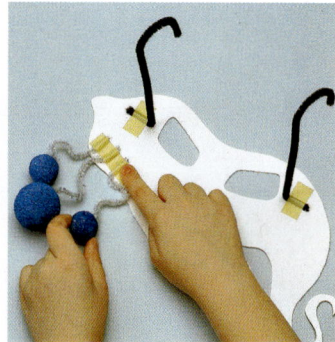

3 Decorate your fish with glittery scales made of sequins and sparkles. Pieces of felt cut into wavy shapes make great fins. Simply cut them out and glue them to the mask.

4 Craft foam balls painted blue stand in as bubbles. Stick a pipe cleaner into each ball and tape them to the mask. Two more pipe cleaners secure the mask to the face.

YOU'LL NEED:

Materials:
- Poster board
- Acrylic paint
- Sparkles and sequins
- Craft foam balls

Tools:
- Scissors
- Craft knife
- Paintbrush
- Glue gun

Tips:

- Make eye openings oversized so that you can see clearly.
- Don't wear masks to go out trick-or-treating.

Gallant Knight
Paint the mask (page 31) gray and glue the armored section into place above the eyes. Imitation rivets are a cinch to create with sequins. Staple feathers to the top of mask.

Pumpkin Head
This mask (page 33) can be painted and then decorated with sparkles for a freckled face.

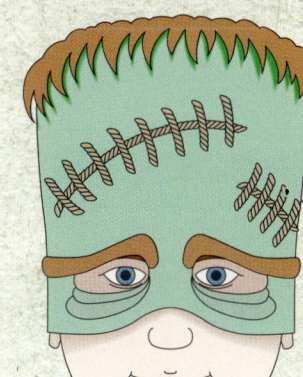

Freaky Frank
Use green paint to give your Frankenstein (page 32) a deathly pallor. Glue on yarn or steel wool for hair and eyebrows. The stitches are made with strands of yarn.

Face Magic

Makeup brings a world of fantastic characters to life. Use water-based cosmetics and check a theatre supplier for special effects including crepe hair for a Bluebeard, tooth black for Captain Hook's front teeth, and glitter gel to brighten the face of your favorite Space Cadet.

Tips:

- Only use cosmetics made exclusively for face painting.
- Test for allergies first by applying a dab to the inside of one wrist.
- Eyes should always be relaxed and closed when painting near them.
- Don't apply glitter gel or metallic powder near eyes.
- Don't use glitter or sequins on very young children.

Whiteface is the base for clowns, vampires, ghouls, and grim reapers. Apply with a damp sponge using long strokes toward the center. One coat does it. A second only goes streaky. Let dry before adding colors.

Removing water-based cosmetics is easy. Just wipe the skin with a damp cloth. Then wash with soap and water.

This little lion's telltale features are her nose and whiskers. Fill in the area above the upper lip and above the eyes with yellow. Using either a paint brush or cotton swabs, paint the whiskers, the nose, and the connecting lines in black. For the rest of her costume, see page 20.

Count Dracula's cloak (page 7)

Count Dracula's ashen face is produced by applying a whiteface base. Darken the eyebrows and paint a widow's peak with black face paint. Spray paint the hair black with colored hair spray. Add the blood red lipstick, stick in some plastic fangs, and you're ready to go.

YOU'LL NEED:

Materials:
- Whiteface performance makeup
- Water-based cosmetics
- Selection of bright colored lipsticks
- Glitter gel

Tools:
- Selection of different sized paintbrushes
- Cotton swabs
- Foam latex cosmetic sponges
- Soap
- Washcloth

Be as goofy as you like when it comes to clowns. Begin with whiteface, let it dry, then use bright colors to paint on exaggerated features. Arch the eyebrows, curl the lips, and don't forget the teardrops. For the rest of her costume, try outsize men's shoes (stuff the toes with paper so they fit), a white men's shirt, suspenders, and a bow tie—polka-dotted, of course!

...Face Magic

Tip: Fix face-painting mistakes by erasing only the part you want to change. Dab a moistened cotton swab on the area, then dry with a fresh swab.

Simple black and white lines combine to make a great spider-web face. After applying a layer of white, brush on seven thick black lines radiating outward from the tip of the nose. Use a smaller brush to create the thin black lines that form the webbing. The final touch—a plastic spider—can be glued on with spirit gum.

This clown face relies on facial features and painted outlines to accentuate colors and shapes. First, ring the blue triangles and yellow star with a contrasting orange line. Paint the nose by following its curves with red, and align the ends of the extended mouth with the outside corners of the eyes. The final touch—a rainbow wig—gives all your colors a knockout punch!

Toddlers without the patience for an extended makeup session will appreciate this quick and easy rabbit face. First, sponge on a light gray wash above the upper lip to create a realistic background for whiskers. Brush the whiskers on by adding black dots and three or four lines on either side. Outline the two rabbit teeth in black below the lower lip, then fill them in with white. Furry fabric ears and a pink triangle nose add final bunny touches.

Tip:

Blend colors together by working in layers. Sponge on the first color. Let it dry. Then with an almost dry sponge, add a deeper or lighter tone, allowing the first color to remain visible.

Just like a real butterfly, this beautiful winged creature begins with a caterpillar body. Start by drawing a black outline of a circle for the head, then add the long body down the center of the nose. Fill in the shape, then add white lines to give it dimension. Test your artistic flair by adding the symmetrical spiral antennae, beginning with thick lines, trailing off to thinner ones. Outline the upper wings in orange, the lower ones in purple, then fill in the shapes with lighter colors applied with a sponge. Add the wing spots after the base colors have dried. For an added iridescent effect, brush on makeup glitter.

Show a sensitive side to Halloween with this sad Pierrot. The white bathing cap not only keeps hair clear of the face paint, but lets the eyes, mouth, and stark coloring stand out. Paint on short blue-black rays to accentuate the eyes. Extend the center portion of the mouth in red to create a pouting expression. Finally, apply the single large tear in deep blue, then highlight it in a lighter tone.

To find just the right ghoulish tone for Frankenstein's skin, experiment with mixtures of green, yellow, and blue. Cover the face and ears by sponging on the chosen mixture. Deepen eye sockets with dark blue or purple. Brush on the head scar and lips in a deep ochre, then add creases and cracks in dried-blood red. For some extra-gory detail, add more dripping blood to the corner of the mouth. Heavy black eyebrows, applied with a thick brush, increase the visual weight of the head, which is crowned with a mop of gelled hair.

Heads & Tails

Ears and a tail—ably assisted by dramatic makeup (page 16)—are all that are needed to carry out the magical transformation from human to beast. We went a step further with this lovely lion, dressing her for a cool Halloween evening in a body suit made out of thick fleece—cut to her shape and glued along the seams. But a sweat suit would have sufficed.

YOU'LL NEED:

Materials:
- Thick fleece
- Synthetic fur
- Wire
- Pipe cleaners
- Ribbon
- Craft fill

Tools:
- Scissors
- Glue gun

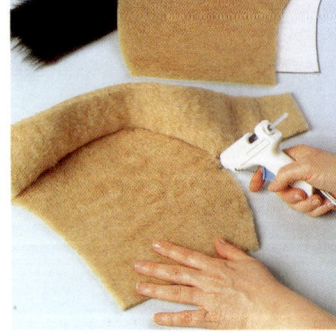

1 Make a hood of thick fleece by gluing together the pieces you cut using the pattern on page 29. Keep the right sides (the side of the fabric you want on the outside) together as you glue.

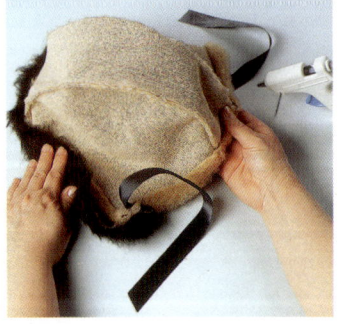

2 Trim with synthetic fur. Glue two ribbons to the sides of the hat. Turn the hood right side out.

20

Tip:

One way to attach a tail is to cut a hole in a piece of fabric, pull one end of the tail through, and glue it on the inside. Then secure the fabric to the seat of your pants with safety pins.

3 For ears, cut four fleece pieces using the lion ear pattern on page 29. Glue two pieces, right sides together, and let dry. Repeat for the second ear. Turn the ears right side out. Bend two pipe cleaners into U-shapes and insert them into the pockets for shape. Fill with craft fill and glue to the hood.

4 For a long tail, cut out a piece of fabric at least 6" (152mm) wide. Fold in half lengthwise, right sides together, and glue to form a tube. Turn the tube right side out.

5 Glue a piece of synthetic fur to one end. Insert a piece of wire the length of the tail. It should be bent at one end and looped at the other. Stuff the tail with craft fill. Seal it closed and glue it to the back of the costume.

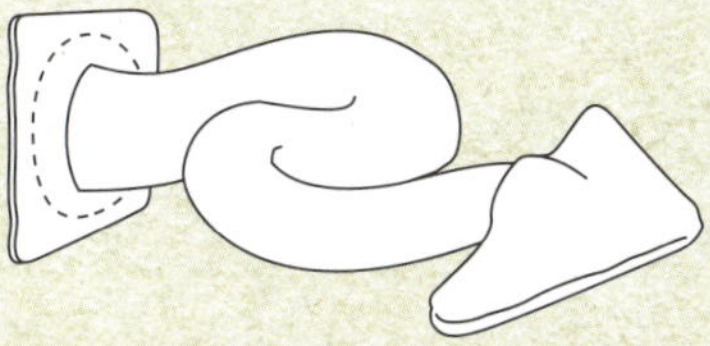

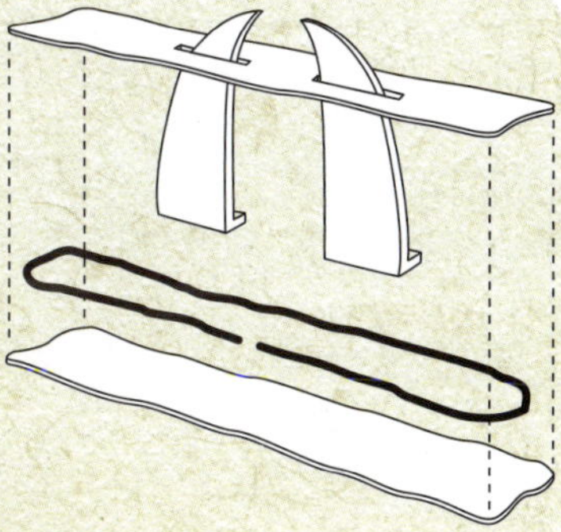

Devil

Poster board horns protrude through slits in the top layer of a fabric headband stiffened with wire. For the tail, stuff a long red or black stocking and glue a triangle of felt to one end. Cut out a pitchfork (also poster board) and wrap it in aluminum foil.

Rabbit

Make ears and headband from poster board and a fluffy tail with cotton wool and fabric. Draw big bunny teeth and whiskers on your face. Don't forget to carry a carrot!

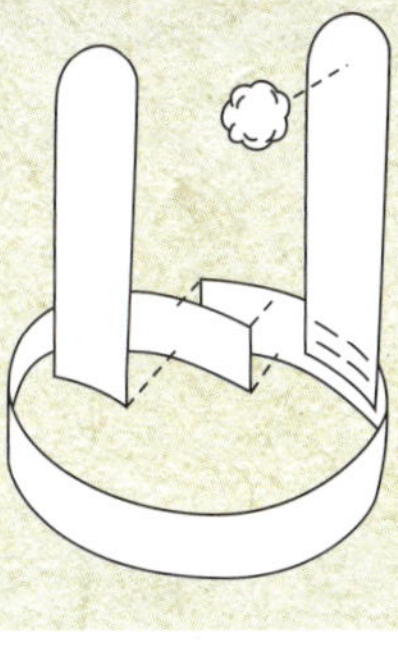

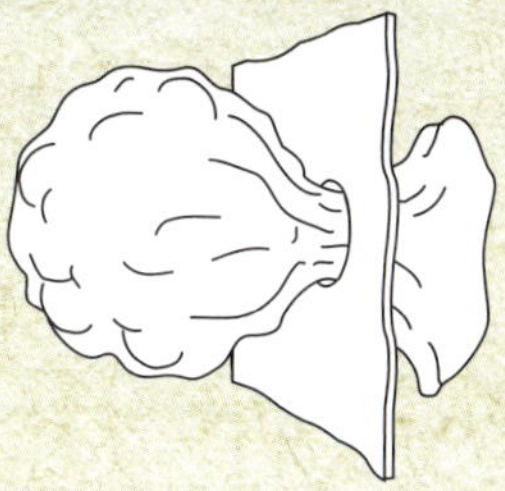

Winged Wonders

The paper wings for this divine creature are made with wire and natural fiber wrapping paper. Modify the shape of the wings and use different kinds of fabric and paper and you'll come up with any number of winged wonders. Then make the wings your very own by your personal choice of decorations.

YOU'LL NEED:

Materials:
- Natural fiber wrapping paper
- Wire (18 gauge)
- Wooden dowel
- Garland of stars
- Elastic tape

Tools:
- Pliers
- Glue gun

Tip:
Be careful when working with wire pieces; their ends can poke and scratch.

Our cone hat (page 12) is wrapped in gold fabric and trimmed with a garland of gold stars

Magic wand (page 25)

We found this white cotton cassock—once worn, no doubt, by a young chorister—in our local thrift shop. If you have no such luck, use a white sheet or a length of white fabric. Cut a hole for the head, trim the length, and glue gold trim around the edges.

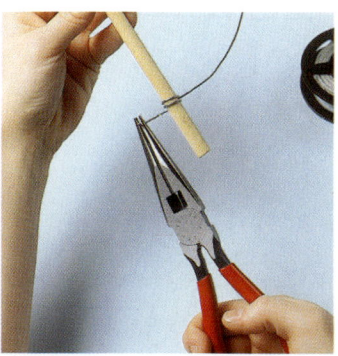

1 Make the wings by bending the wire into the shape you desire. (We used two pieces of wire to create a heart shape for the princess.) Wrap the wire ends around the wooden dowel.

2 Cover the wire frame in wrapping paper (or material) and secure with glue or tape. Flip the wings over and repeat wrap the other side. We glued on a star garland.

3 Cut strips of elastic tape for shoulder straps and glue their ends to the wooden spine. Now you're ready for flight.

Butterfly
Stretch brightly colored cellophane over the wings and then decorate with cutouts of cellophane in contrasting colors. Paint your face (page 19).

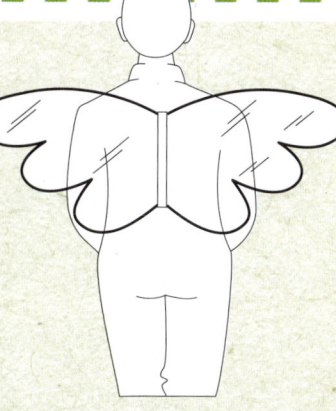

Bird
Wrap the wire frame with a light fabric and glue on an array of feathers. For the beak, consider a mask cut out of poster board and decorated with more feathers.

Bat
Black tulle or other gauzy fabric would create the effect of bat wings. Use the method shown on page 21 to make bat ears and wear a black leotard and stockings.

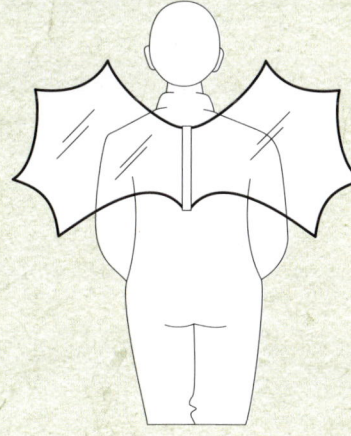

Dragonfly
Transparent cellophane suggests the delicacy needed for dragonfly wings. For antennae, stick craft foam balls to the ends of two pieces of wire, which are wrapped around a headband.

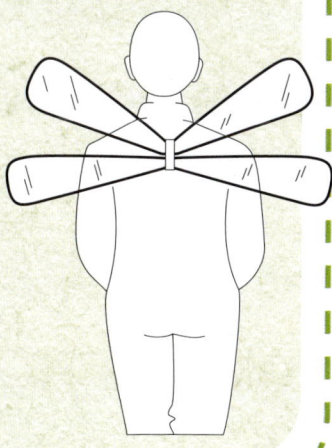

Tools of the Trade

What's a pirate without a hook, a knight without a sword, or a fairy without a magic wand? The right accessory can transform a collection of old clothes into a convincing costume. Don't forget your local thrift store. While you're not likely to find a magic wand there, you might discover a battered violin case, long satin gloves, a butterfly net, some truly outstanding pieces of costume jewelry, the absolutely perfect set of opera glasses…

Cutlass

Cut the blade from foamcore and the basket and grip from craft foam sheets (patterns, page 27). Spray paint the blade silver. Cut slits in the basket and slide it on the blade. Glue extra bits of foam sheet to both sides of the basket to help keep its shape.

Bow, Arrow, and a Full Quiver

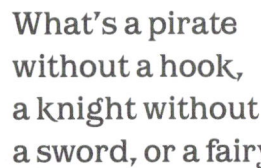

Notches for holding the string secure are the key to a great bow. For the rest of Robin Hood's attire see page 9.

Sword

Foamcore makes a perfect sword (pattern, page 27.) Paint it silver and use an aluminum plate for the basket. For the rest of the knight's garb see page 8.

The quiver was made out of a poster tube wrapped in a thin layer of cork. The arrows are wood dowels topped with feathers from a duster and secured to the inside of the quiver with glue.

Shield

We cut a 20" x 24" (508 x 610mm) piece of foamcore into the shape of a shield. The handles (hidden in back) are made with elastic tape like those for the wing's shoulder straps (page 23, step 3).

Blue plastic plate with a plastic canvas for embroidery glued to the bottom.

Aluminum foil

Pipe cleaners

Ribbon

Magic Wand

We made the star with a piece of wire. After gluing paper to the wire and gluing the wire to the end of a wooden dowel, we painted the whole thing gold and added a trim of gold pipe cleaners. For the rest of the divine costume see page 22.

Hook Hand

The hook is a plastic clothes hanger passed through a hole cut in the bottom of a yogurt container wrapped in aluminum foil. If you use a wire hanger, make sure you wrap the ends in electric tape. For the rest of the pirate costume see page 4.

Starstruck Clown

All this clown needed to get in the mood was an oversized bow tie, makeup, and an arrow through his head. We used craft foam for the arrowhead and for the fletching. To make the arrow, cut a wooden dowel in half, twist the ends of a piece of wire around the free ends of the two rods, and bend the wire to curve over the shape of the head. For cushioning, slip on a couple of craft foam rings or latex washers.

Patterns

Tip:

To make really gigantic patterns, photocopy the pattern as large as you can. Cut it out. Hang an enormous piece of white paper (such as pattern paper available in fabric stores) on the wall. In a darkened room hold the pattern between a lit lamp and the wall, while a helper outlines the silhouette on the paper. Remove the paper from the wall and cut out the enlarged pattern.

Here are the patterns to help you complete some of the costumes and props in this book. We used a grid of ½" (13mm) squares for our patterns and for each one we have provided the figure you need to enlarge it to the size we used. Use a photocopier or the grid method to ensure the enlarged pattern is proportionate. Once you have determined the size you want (e.g., graph paper with 1" (25mm) squares for a 200% enlargement, or graph paper with 2" (51mm) squares for a 400% enlargement), copy the pattern, square by square, onto your graph paper, following the same angles and curves. Tape the enlarged pattern to the surface of the material you plan to use and cut around it with scissors or a craft knife.

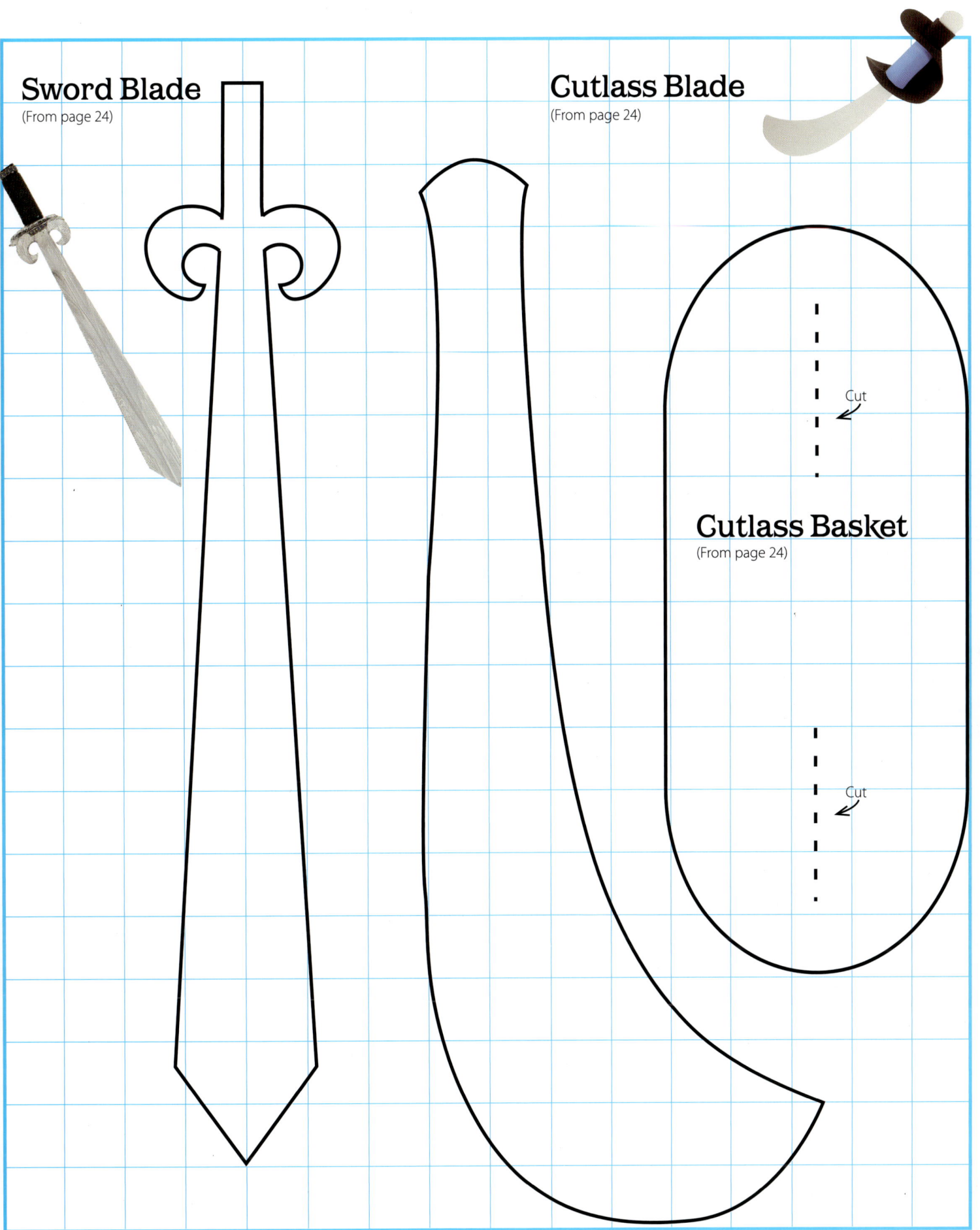

Sword Blade
(From page 24)

Cutlass Blade
(From page 24)

Cutlass Basket
(From page 24)

Cut

Cut

Enlarge 200% (1" squares)   Enlarge 400% (2" squares)

27

Robin Hood's Cap

(From page 13)

- Photocopy this page at 170%.
- Cut out the patterns.
- For the crown, fold a piece of felt (measuring at least 12" x 24" [305mm x 610mm]) widthwise. Place the crown pattern on the felt with the back along the fold. Cut out the crown. Glue the top and front together.
- For the brim, fold a second piece of felt (measuring at least 12" x 12" [305mm x 305mm]) in half. Place the brim pattern on the felt with the front along the fold. Cut out the brim. Glue the ends of the brim together, then glue it to the bottom edge of the crown. Turn the cap right side out.

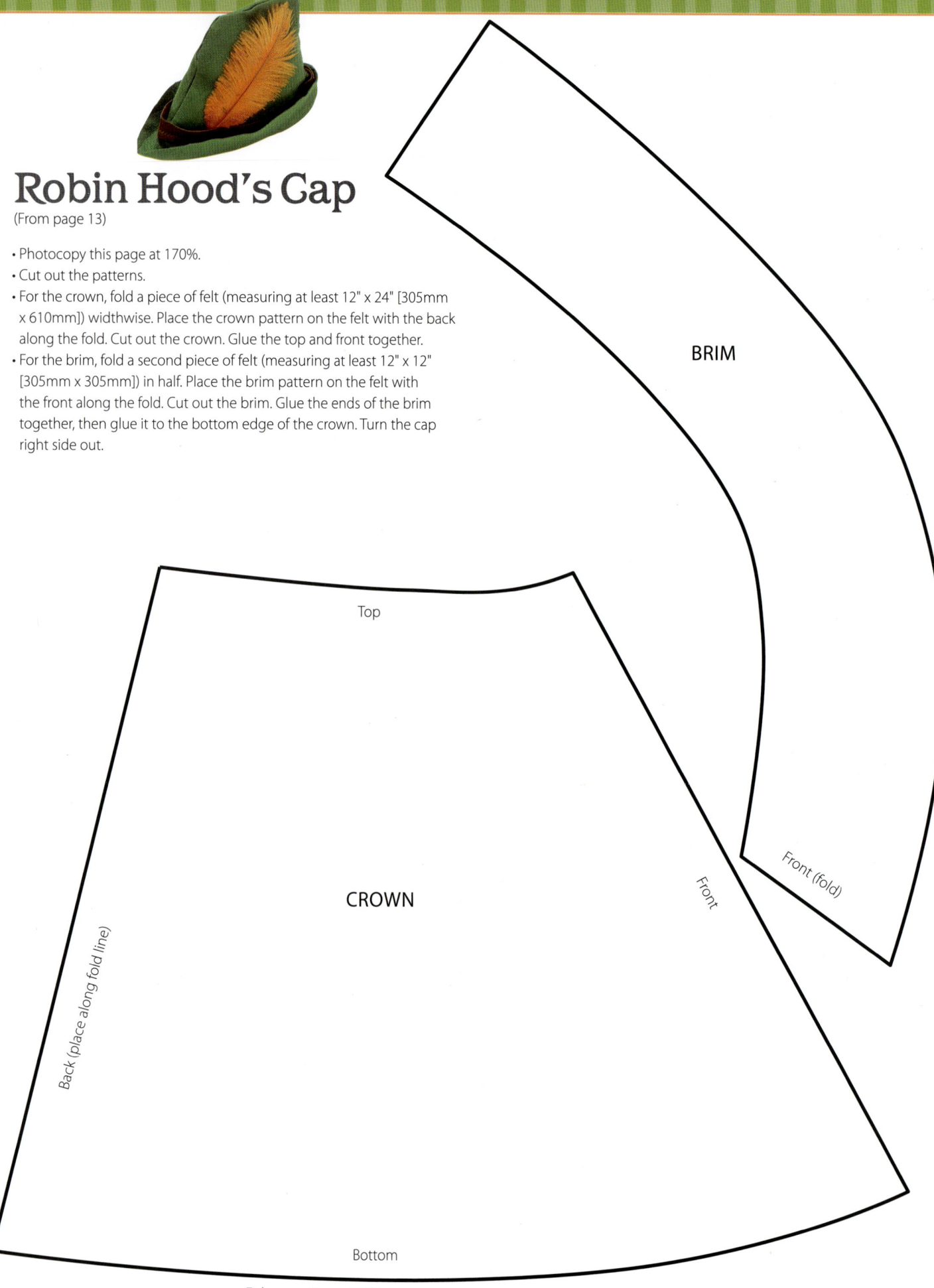

Enlarge patterns 170%

Lion's Hood

(From page 20)

- Make a photocopy of this page.
- Cut out the patterns.
- Make 2 photocopies of the side flap at 180%.
- Make 4 photocopies of the ear at 180%.
- Cut the crown piece in half. Photocopy each half at 180%. Tape the halves together.
- Cut fabric, using the patterns.
- Glue the side flaps to the crown, making a hood.
- Make the ears and glue them to the top of the hood.

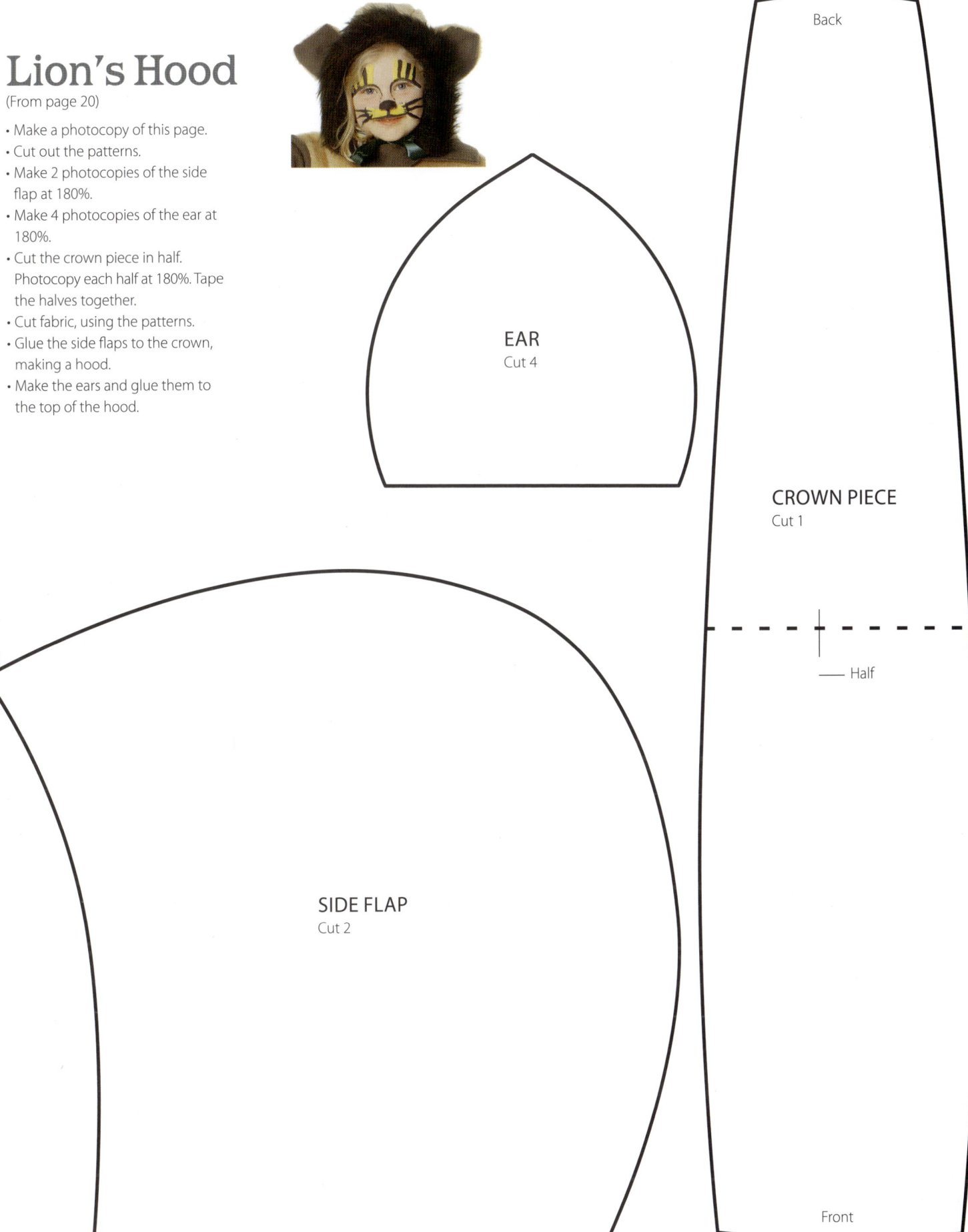

EAR
Cut 4

CROWN PIECE
Cut 1

Back

Half

Front

SIDE FLAP
Cut 2

Enlarge patterns 180%

Mask Parade
(From page 14)

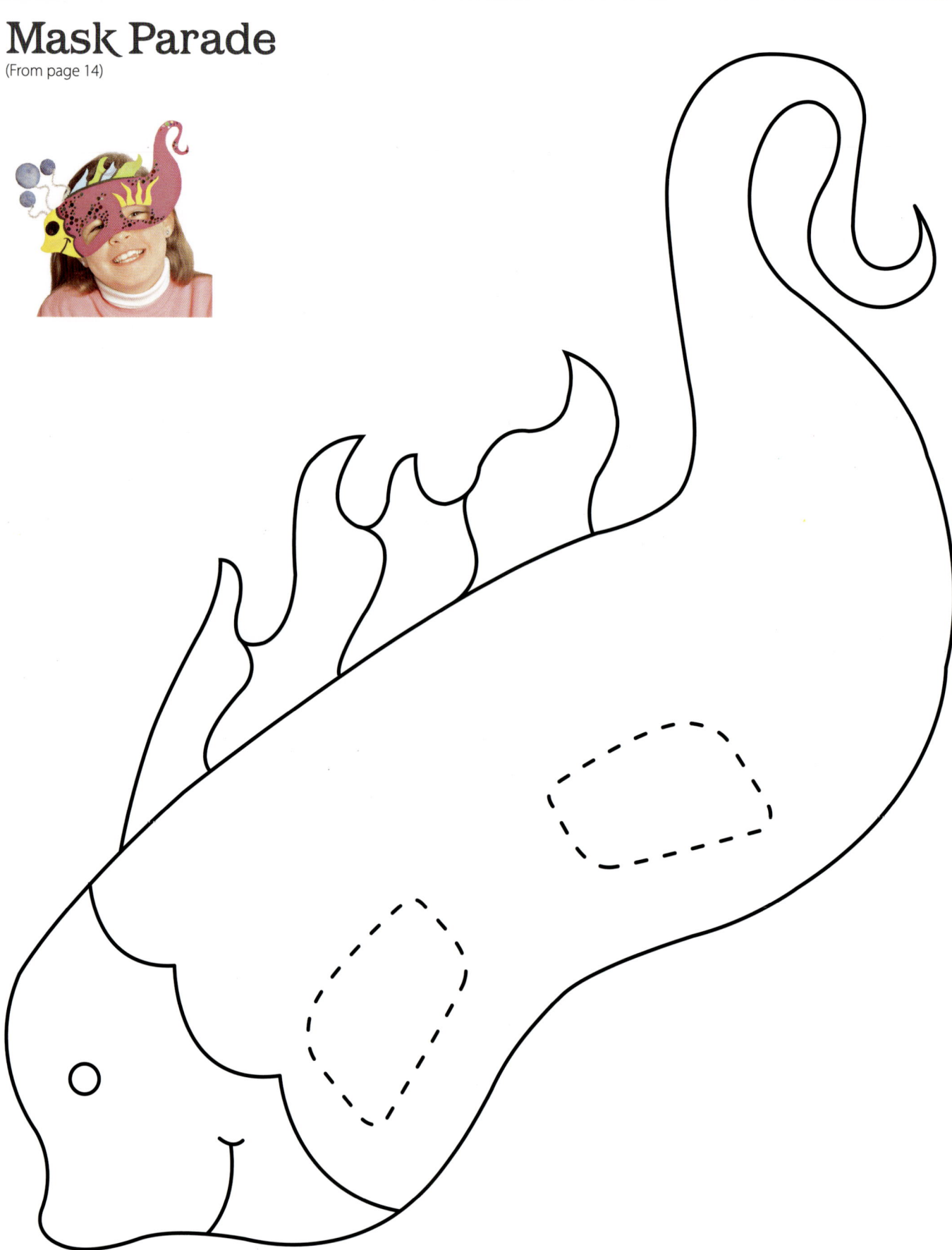

Scale pattern to fit face

Mask Parade
(From page 15)

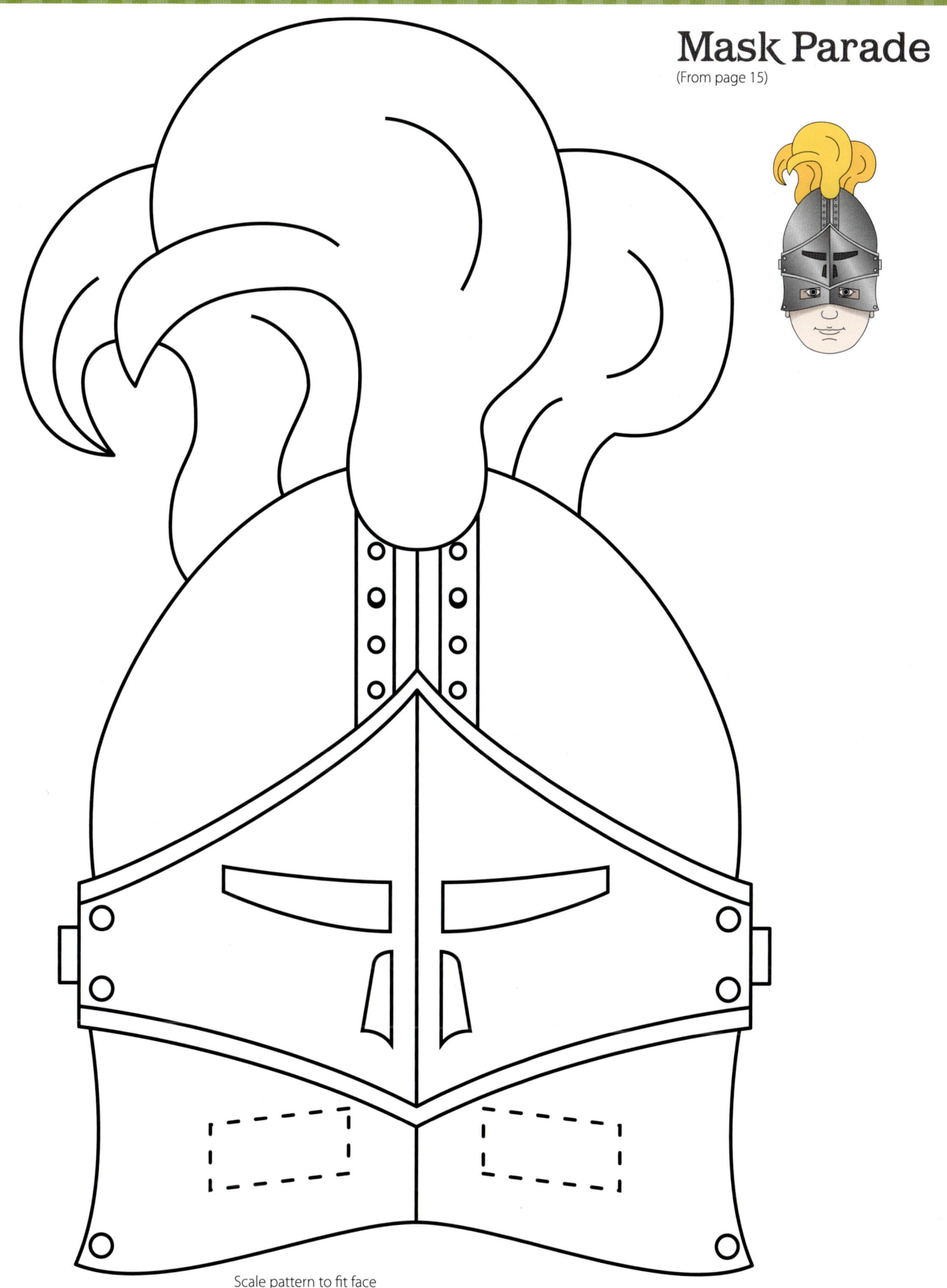

Scale pattern to fit face

31

Mask Parade
(From page 15)

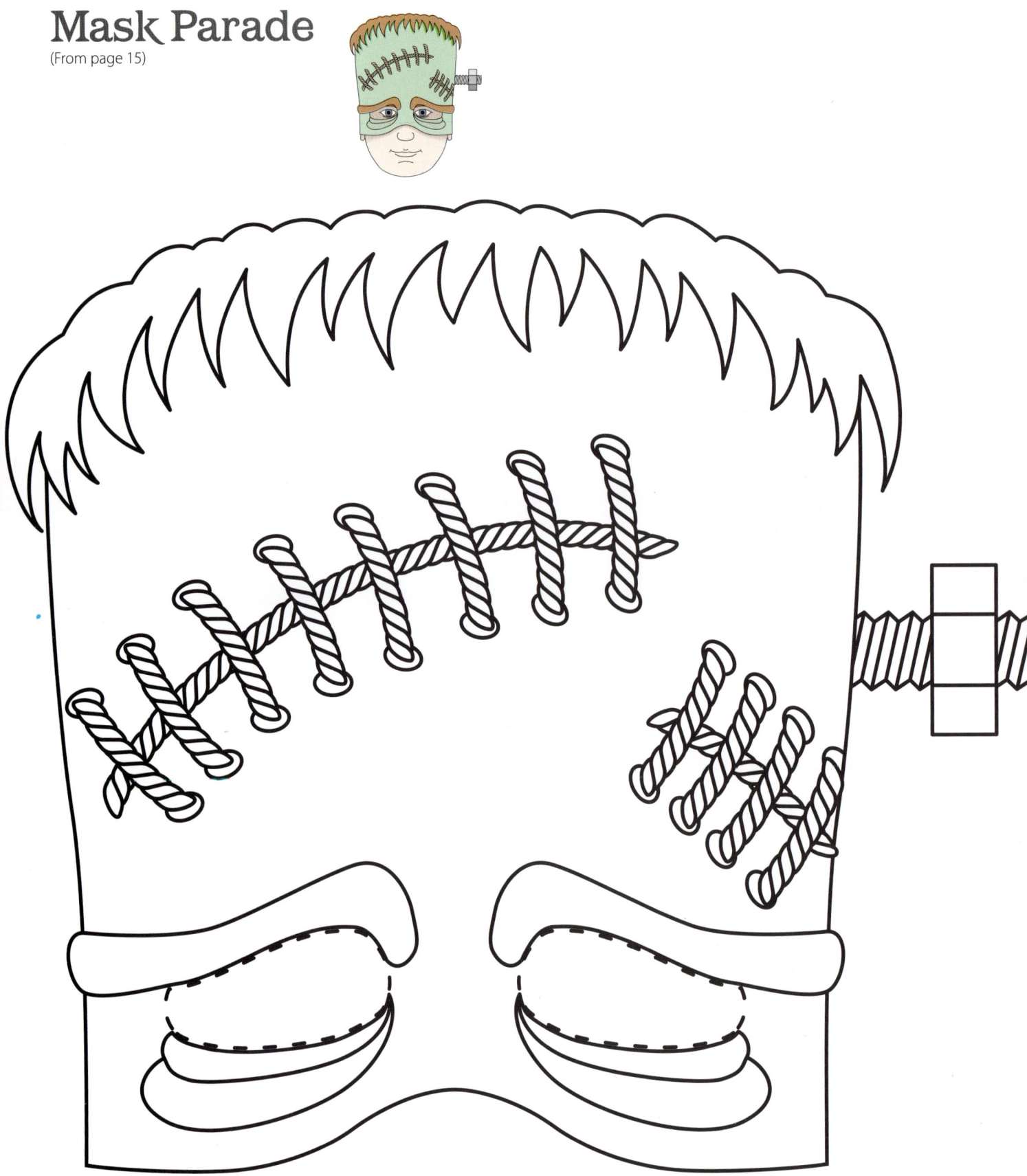

Scale pattern to fit face

Mask Parade
(From page 15)

Scale pattern to fit face

33

More Great Project Books from Design Originals

Pumpkin Patch
Carving, Painting & Unique Techniques To Inspire Your Halloween Spirit
By Suzanne McNeill

26 great patterns and loads of tips for awesome jack-o-lantern fun!

ISBN: 978-1-57421-274-7
DO3397
$7.99 • 24 Pages

Zentangle® for Kidz
A Comic Guide with Alex and Lilah
By Sandy Steen Bartholomew

Kids of all ages can learn that it's easy to tangle in this fun presentation of pattern play.

ISBN: 978-1-57421-340-9
DO3463
$8.99 • 16 Pages

Friendship Bracelets 102
Friendship Know No Boundaries… Over 50 Bracelets To Make & Share
By Suzanne McNeill

Included are techniques with easy knots and simple wheel weaving methods to make friendship bracelets.

ISBN: 978-1-57421-294-5
DO3442
$8.99 • 16 Pages

Strings 'N Things
Fun & Cool Craft Projects for Kids & Teens!
By Suzanne McNeill

Encourage children to create a variety of beautifully decorated items that will inspire them to explore their own creativity and expand their interest in crafting.

ISBN: 978-1-57421-293-8
DO3441
$8.99 • 16 Pages

Just Like Me Crochet Patterns
Quick-and-Easy Projects for American Girls and Their 18" Dolls
By Cony Larsen

This booklet is a handy guide for girls of all ages who want to learn to crochet. Beginners will get started in just minutes with easy-to-complete projects.

ISBN: 978-1-57421-347-8
DO3470
$12.99 • 24 Pages

Poms, Stems and Wiggles
Fun Projects For Kids And Groups
By Linda Valentino

Make your gathering more festive with these creative projects.

ISBN: 978-1-57421-292-1
DO3440
$8.99 • 16 Pages

Big Bold Beads
Fun Projects for Boys and Girls
By Suzanne McNeill

From bracelets and baubles, to flip flops and keychains, these projects promise hours of fun.

ISBN: 978-1-57421-328-7
DO3451
$8.99 • 16 Pages

The New Look For Styrofoam
By Andrea Gibson

Decorate your home with style and imaginative art, with crafts made from Styrofoam.

ISBN: 978-1-57421-311-9
DO3409
$7.99 • 16 Pages

Look for These Books at Your Local Bookstore or Specialty Retailer
To order direct, call 800-457-9112 or visit www.d-originals.com
By mail, please send check or money order + S&H to:
Fox Chapel Publishing, 1970 Broad Street, East Petersburg, PA 17520

# Item	US Shipping Rate
1 Item	$3.25
Each Additional	.25

Canadian & International Orders – please email d-originals.com@ foxchapelpublishing.com or visit our website for actual shipping costs.